First World War
and Army of Occupation
War Diary
France, Belgium and Germany

55 DIVISION
166 Infantry Brigade,
Brigade Trench Mortar Battery
2 March 1916 - 20 April 1916

WO95/2930/3

The Naval & Military Press Ltd
www.nmarchive.com
Published in association with The National Archives

Published by

The Naval & Military Press Ltd

Unit 10 Ridgewood Industrial Park,

Uckfield, East Sussex,

TN22 5QE England

Tel: +44 (0) 1825 749494

www.naval-military-press.com

www.nmarchive.com

This diary has been reprinted in facsimile from the original. Any imperfections are inevitably reproduced and the quality may fall short of modern type and cartographic standards.

© **Crown Copyright**
Images reproduced by permission of The National Archives, London, England, 2015.

Contents

Document type	Place/Title	Date From	Date To
Heading	WO95/2930/3 166 Infantry Bde Brigade Trench Mortar Battery Mar 1916-Aug 1916		
Heading	55th Division 166th Infy Bde 166th Lt Trench Mortar Bty 1916 Mar-Aug 1916		
War Diary		02/03/1916	20/04/1916
Heading	166th Brigade 55th Division 166th Light Trench Mortar Battery June & July 1916		
War Diary		00/06/1916	00/06/1916
Heading	War Diary Of The 166th Brigade Trench Mortar Battery 55th (West Lancashire) Division For The Period 1st July 1916 To 31st July 1916 Vol 4		
War Diary		00/07/1916	00/07/1916
Heading	166th Brigade 55th Division 166th Light Trench Mortar Battery August 1916		
Heading	War Diary Of The 166th Trench Mortar Battery For The Period 1st August To 31st August 1916 Vol 5		
War Diary		00/08/1916	00/08/1916

WO95/2930/2

166 INFANTRY BDE

BRIGADE TRENCH MORTAR BATTERY
MAR 1916 - AUG 1916

55TH DIVISION
166TH INFY BDE

166TH LT TRENCH MORTAR BTY

1916 MAR ~~JUN~~ - AUG 1916

WAR DIARY
or
INTELLIGENCE SUMMARY
(Erase heading not required.)

Army Form C. 2118

Instructions regarding War Diaries and Intelligence Summaries are contained in F.S. Regs., Part II. and the Staff Manual respectively. Title Pages will be prepared in manuscript.

166/1/TM

Place	Date	Hour	Summary of Events and Information	Remarks and references to Appendices
			The Battery returned from 3rd Army School of Trench Mortars on Thursday night 2nd March 1916 and was stationed at GROSVILLE being known as The 421 Trench Mortar Batty 2nd Lt J. H. GARDINER 5 King's Own Regt being in Command with 2nd Lt M. WAYMAN 5 South Lanc's Regt as second in Command. The Batty consists of 4 guns. (registered numbers 187 - 196 - 241 - 299) 3 in⁵ QF MARK I STOKES HOWITZER	
	Satʲ. 4/3/16		Battery inspected by BRIGADIER GENERAL WILKINSON.	
	Tuesday 7/3/16		2nd Lt J. H GARDINER on being transferred to the 8/Bth King's Own Regt left the Batty - the Command of the Batty then falling on 2nd Lt M. WAYMAN who was joined by 2nd Lt E. V. POPE 5th King's Own Regt.	
	Friday 10.3.16		201 Rounds of Ammunition received and 3 Rounds were fired at 400yds range to demonstrate the gun to BRIGADIER GENERAL WILKINSON in the afternoon.	
	Satʲ 11.3.16		Prepared an emplacement to fire from in The GRANGE	
	Sunday 12.3.16		Fired 9 Rounds from emplacement in The GRANGE	
	Tuesday 14.3.16		2nd Lt E. V. POPE wound his Regt and was succeeded by 2nd Lt E. H. TAYLOR 5th Loyal North LANCS Regt.	
	Wedʲ 15.3.16		6 men from 5 South LANCS Regt arrived for 7 days course of instruction	

WAR DIARY
or
INTELLIGENCE SUMMARY

(Erase heading not required.)

Army Form C. 2118

Place	Date	Hour	Summary of Events and Information	Remarks and references to Appendices
			Saty 18.3.16 2 guns taken to the Trenches and 18 Rounds fired from positions in The GRANGE and The WILLOWS - Instructions received that in future the Batty will be known as 166/1 Trench Mortar Batty.	
			Monday 20.3.16 One gun taken up to the Trenches and 12 Rounds fired from a Sap in The GRANGE. 3 men of the Batty left to join the 5th Batty (Mortars) Special Brigade of R.E.	
			Wednesday 22/3/16 "Stand to" received at 10.25 P.M. and Batty reported present to move off at 10.45 P.M. 6 men from 5 Loyal North Lancs Regt joined for a 7 days course of instruction.	
			Thursday 23.3.16 One gun fired 6 Rounds from The GRANGE Trenches	
			Monday 27.3.16 One gun taken to The WILLOWS and 6 rounds fired	
			Tuesday 28.3.16 55th Divisional Order No 401(9) received ordering "Stokes" Trench Mortars are not to be employed in the front line	

MMurray 2nd Lt
O.C. 166/1 Trench Mortar Bty
31.3.16.

Army Form C. 2118

WAR DIARY of 166/1 Trench Mortar Batty.
or
INTELLIGENCE SUMMARY for April 1916

(Erase heading not required.)

Instructions regarding War Diaries and Intelligence Summaries are contained in F.S. Regs., Part II. and the Staff Manual respectively. Title Pages will be prepared in manuscript.

Place	Date	Hour	Summary of Events and Information	Remarks and references to Appendices
	3rd April 1916.		Notified by 166 Infantry Brigade that the Battery would be temporarily attached to 165 Brigade	
	4th April 1916.		The Battery moved from GROSVILLE to WAILLEY at 7.30pm.	
	5th April 1916.		First days firing done in 165th Brigade area.	
	10th April 1916.		First night firing done by the Batty.	
	15th April 1916		The Batty got into a very warm corner, being under continuous hot German artillery fire for one hour. The periscope was smashed in two, the legs of the tripod of gun No 299 got slightly damaged, the elevating gear clipped before the gun could be got under cover. Later in the day the Batty from another emplacement retaliated on the Saps heads serving up over 52 rounds	
	20th April 1916.		165/1. Trench Mortar Batty. joined the Brigade it was received to have the Brigade front between 166/1. & 165/2 Trench Mortar Batty. The 166th Batty taking the left half of the front. During the greater part of the month the weather was cold and wet only taking up at and after Easter. From the 8th to 30th inst the Batty fired 150 rounds.	

M. Wayman 2nd Lt.
O.C. 166/1 Trench Mortar Batty.
April 1916.

Army Form C. 2118

WAR DIARY
or
INTELLIGENCE SUMMARY of 166/1 Trench Mortar Batty.
for May 1916.

(Erase heading not required.)

Place	Date	Hour	Summary of Events and Information	Remarks and references to Appendices

The Battery continued to be attached to 165 Brigade at WAILLY and during the month of MAY fired 157 rounds dispersing working parties - silencing Machine guns - and helping to keep in subjection the 11 Japs on the Brigade front. On SATURDAY. MAY. 22 The Batty made every arrangement to put up a barrage for a raiding party under Capt'n MOTTRAM of the 7th Bat'n Kings LIVERPOOL Reg't. but at the last moment the raid was put off.

M. Wayman.
Lieut
O/C. 166/1 T.M.B'ty.

166th Brigade.

55th Division.

L -----

166th LIGHT TRENCH MORTAR BATTERY

JUNE & JULY 1916

Army Form C. 2118.

WAR DIARY
or
INTELLIGENCE SUMMARY of 166/1 Trench Mortar Batty.
for June 1916

(Erase heading not required.)

The Batty has remained at NAILLY under the 165 Infantry Brigade. On the 3rd/4th inst the Batty took part in supplying barrage for an attempted raid, organised by the 5th Batt. Liverpool Regt. Fire opened at 12.56 AM for 2 mins from the 24th mounds. The Batty has been engaged in active co-operation bombarding the enemy front line daily. Total rounds fired for the month 1641.
One Officer 2 Corporals + 20 other ranks receiving wounds and one Other rank killed in action.
Operations are still in progress.

M. Wayman. Lieut
r.c. Batty.

War Diary
of the
166th Brigade Trench Mortar Battery
55th (West Lancashire) Division
for the period
1st July, 1916 to 31st July, 1916.

WAR DIARY or INTELLIGENCE SUMMARY of 166 T.M. Bty for July 1916. Army Form C. 2118

The Batty finished the 8th day of the Operations carried out by 165 Brigade on 1st inst at WAILLY firing 300 rounds in that day. On the 10th inst No 7 Section put up a successful barrage for a raid on Sap F at WAILLY carried out by the 7th Batt'n King's Liverpool Regt. On the 12th No 7 Section moved to AGNY to work under 166 Brigade. No 2 Section being at GOUY resting. On the 14th inst at 3 A.M. in accordance with Operation orders No 71. Rotow fire was opened recommenced till 3.45 A.M. when the rate was increased till 4 A.M. The Batty remained at AGNY till 1 am 20th inst returning from whence fired 2417 rounds Successfully putting out of action a machine gun on the 16th inst. from AGNY the Batty retired the 166 Brigade on the march 1st to the end of the month halting at GRAND RULLÉCOURT, LUCHEUX - LE MEILLARD. BEAUMETZ. CANDAS where it entrained for the ANCRE VALLEY.

M Trayner Capt
O.C. Batty

166th Brigade.
55th Division,

166th LIGHT TRENCH MORTAR BATTERY

AUGUST 1 9 1 6

166 T.M. Bty
Vol 5

War Diary
of the
166th Trench Mortar Battery
for the period
1st August to 31st August
1916.

WAR DIARY or INTELLIGENCE SUMMARY

Army Form C. 2118.

7 (16 T A) Bty
33rd Division — 1st Aug 1916

Place	Date	Hour	Summary of Events and Information	Remarks and references to Appendices

On the 17th Augt the Batty left the Bivouac at MANSEL COPSE for Quarters at TALUS BOIS where it remained till the 5th Augt when it returned to bivouac till the evening when we were ordered to go up for an attack on GUILLEMONT. On the 9th 2nd Lt R H TAYLOR and one other rank were wounded. Returned to the bivouac on the 10th and Lieut R H TAYLOR fell recovering on the 12th. The Batty returned to 5 T M By on the 11th Augt. We had a very heavy barrage when relaying the relief. Stay the Batty was guarding our BARRIER on the left and half in Assembly Trench on the right. Twenty rounds of the Batty were released at 2 am on the 19th by G.O. Brigade THB and the night day of the Raid we under at 11pm on the 15th by 25th Brigade THB. The Batty moved to Huts at MEAULTE the same day. Saty 19th Augt the Batty returned at EDGE HILL Station to MARTINVILLE and marched to Huts at FRESSENNEVILLE. Training only. Command of Bde passed on 29th to moved to ERCOURT.

More than the Batty moved with 16th Brigade to the area of the XV Corps.

M Way (signed)
O.C. Batty

www.ingramcontent.com/pod-product-compliance
Lightning Source LLC
Chambersburg PA
CBHW081513160426
43193CB00014B/2680